Welcome *to* Flowerville:

Poetry *from* San Juan Commons

by Robin Ray

Welcome *to* Flowerville: Poetry *from* San Juan Commons

by Robin Ray

© 2019 Robin Ray

All rights reserved. This book or parts thereof may not be reproduced in any form, stored in any retrieval system, or transmitted in any form by any means – electronic, mechanical, photocopy, recording, or otherwise – without prior written permission of the publisher, except as provided by the United States of America copyright law. For permission requests, write to the publisher, at redrobin62@yahoo.com.

Visit the author's website @
https://seattlewordsmith.wordpress.com/

All photography *by* Robin Ray

Cover Drawing *from* pinestateflowers.com

About the Author clipart *from* pinterest.com.au

To Pamela Ekrem,
Flower Architect *of* San Juan Commons
Port Townsend, WA

Love is *like* a beautiful flower which I may *not* touch, but whose fragrance
makes *the* garden a place *of* delight just *the* same.

Helen Keller

Other Books *by* the Author

SHORT STORY COLLECTIONS
Wetland *and* Other Stories
Obey *the* Darkness: Horror Stories

NOVELS
Commoner *the* Vagabond
Murder *in* Rock & Roll Heaven

NOVELLAS
Stranded *in* Paradise
Iron Maiden
Tears *of* A Clown
Strung Out

NON-FICTION
You Can't Sleep Here: A Clown's Guide *to* Surviving Homelessness

TABLE *of* CONTENTS

The Painting..1

She..2

Box *of* Notes...3

Impressionist Music...................................5

Limb *from* Stoic Limb................................7

Victims...8

Yellow Leaf...9

Last Knight..10

Behind, Between, Believe.............................11

Against *the* Pole...................................12

Out *and* In...14

Betrayed...15

Content..17

Art..19

Palm Jewel...21

Walls..23

The View *from* Taksim Square........................24

What Use Have I?.....................................26

Rude Impermanence....................................27

Where's *the* Rise & Shine Brew?.....................29

About *the* Author...................................30

The Painting

I've begged the print from off your wall, a sturdy, hellebore scene of fall because I stood before it, weak and flushed, with thoughts I've feared to bawl. I've listened to your graven tongue, it breaks and breathes to everyone, and like an owl who's lost its beak I hunger for the work to come. Yet, you assure me, I've devised some way to keep me satisfied, but if I falter, am I weak or just a patron mesmerized, bright colors oozed from artful eyes?

She

She has a life all her own. Can be touched, felt, tickled, or simply left alone from our careless abandon. She cannot be defined by inches or meters, neither can her undulating form be bottled or sold without discretion. She is a unifying force, a carrier of armies, a womb of lives unknown. In front of her, you are tiny alliums, miniscule super pools. Above her, like an endless pillow, a cushion. She is a comforting embrace. Within your reef, a swill of marine souls teem, burst into an epiphany of sorts. I am her watcher; she has a life all her own. Tomorrow, we'll all human again.

Box of Notes

Father knocks the stuffing from his aged pipe into a bowl, a cherrywood clamshell of bright, hypnotizing, iridescent hues screaming, *pick me up!* Laying in his favorite chair, he closes his eyes, soaks in the lavender of invisibly streaming from a condenser on the flowered wall. Quietly, I sit cross-legged on the carpet just a few feet away and plug in the new guitar he'd bought me, plectrum in hand, tubes warming. I give the instrument a casual strum; nothing special, just a desultory caress. Father smiles, looks over. Encouraged, I coax more notes from the strings, channeling the tireless efforts of the celebrated masters.

It isn't long before I fall for the gentle subterfuge of my own imagined greatness. Images swirl in my mind of Hendrix, Blackmore. The frenzied dashes of Zappa alight on the fret board as I careen from score to score, juxtaposing rhythms like Scott Joplin in minstrelsy. Father stands up, walks over. The smile that once laid bare on a face so kind now replaced with an ominous twist of malevolence. This is no ornery ghost in the strand. Is my ashen box of wires too loud in aggressive overtones? I receive no answer, just a simple flick of the switch and all dies. I force no argument, no ruse of the tongue, no ill-borne spirit tugging at bald flesh. After all, he bought it. My gift is silence if he wishes an exchange.

Impressionist Music

At the hands of a skilled pianist, the cascaded waterfall that is Debussy, Ravel, Faure and Dukas, empties into a gently flowing brook. The tapping of the keys, sonorous to the ear, is unstoppable, resilient in its forward momentum. Flowing ghostlike over the fritillaria, I hear the rhythm, fear no tango, the sensitivity of joy corrupting me. I listen as the tones are interrupted ever so slightly by an acorn falling from its lofty perch, a trout struggling against the upstream, unafraid.

There's a young boy skipping flat stones along its calming waves, skipping history through its iridescent shell. This music is an infectious thrust surrendered to mankind by Grecian Muses with nothing else to bestow but what they've loved. Infinite, pregnant with reason, it is thrilling, a gentle fairytale touch, comforting in ways no wooded forest or spectacular rainbow could ever imagine. I let the vibrantly cascading waterfall that is *Le Tombeau de Couperin* wrap me in its tentacles and rejoice. No resistance, no painful sorrow, only spun notes wafting miraculously through my garden.

Limb from Stoic Limb

Nightmares? You speak to me of nightmares, the frosty sparkle of awakenings? It's me when the windflowers of my memory become unbearable; both of us, a pride of agony, restless in our myth. Nothing less than a sledgehammer to our bulging skulls eases the endless suffering. That is *my* nightmare, a tincture of abandon in the wheat.

Victims

Dreams left undreamt, tales left untold, lives left unlived, lovers left to hold. The poppies flood the broken streets with blossomed saints arranged to meet amidst the carousels of doom and cast aside the differences that plagued us from an angry womb. It shall not reek, that scent of the untarnished. It shall not burn, the souls amongst the banished. But a reminder that we, the living, should cherish what we've conquered. It makes us bold enough to dream and dares to make us stronger.

Yellow Leaf

This you know: I am broken, torn, ragdoll innocent, snipped wings that cannot fly and hands which cannot heal. But I aspire like a zephyr in flight to reunite those modern instincts supremely torn asunder and left for dead. Forlornly, I cradle these angry weeds, decaying phlox struggling for air, and my head is filled with insane, and my pride wanton, and lost is forgiven. I am the one who forgives me when forgiving you.

Last Knight

Come hither, steel-formed hero. Be the panacea from my deathbed, my last comfort. My ebbing life, cold, bitter and transparent, flails as it surrenders to shortened infinity. As usual, I forgive the souse asleep in the attic dreaming madness's sober end. Like the piercing call of apathy, my soul, in evanescence to the thin air, withers, fades to a pink petunia's blush. Rapidly, painlessly, I fly - no mountains left to conquer, no sorrows riding high.

Behind, Between, Believe

To our ancestors, the elves that laid our wits to waste, much is owed, and to our progeny, much is revealed. Wisdom is borne on the feeblest of shoulders and the strongest of breastplates. No feast nor flounder of faceless nations ought give vent to our vexing fury, but the simple act, to prosper stubbornly, reveals so much of the pride we contain, wild delphiniums enshrined within as gifts. After the venomous smoke has cleared, we will know from our big hearts come big tales neither of our generations shall forget, thankfully.

Against the Pole

Ready!

He is cruel - more so than I'd been led to believe. Words, like barbed bougainvillea, cut through festering wounds, barely tolerable or required.

Aim!

My blindfold slips. I see the faces pitifully drawn even in withering darkness, this brutal jungle without a name. Perhaps I've lost now but I can take comfort in knowing my cause is far from eulogy.

Fire!

Fear not, my mysterious deliverers, freedom deniers. An old friend arrives in a minute. She was the skintight plant whisperer seducing secrets of nectar. She can sweet you, too.

Out and In

I was a rye-drunk geranium in my dreams, a lonely bicycle begging a rider, one who required no verdict as if his life was on trial. At times, I stood bankrupt, unwove, my missiles dug out, strewn across gasoline plains like the brightest confetti. Someone dared shine a light on the biography of my suicide. This was shocking, then I was joined together again, a vulnerable sprout, bruised, tortured, dusted off, prepared to take those countless lashes again.

Betrayed

Bared to all is this murmuring heart, jagged tongue, a breast heaving the stormy waves of Atlantis. Solace, be her romancer now. Soothe her, let her angry be unlabored like Epimedium dew. A soul betrayed, in need of infirmary, begs triage. With trembling hands, she yearns for the sweet dish best served cold. Jaded by the weak, ill-begotten of the strong, it will be her turn to strike. And like a flame that's sullied the furrowed brow, she will, alone, face the emptying day.

Content

What is content? Is it some illusive beast with stone cold eyes predicating on the weak? Or is it digitalis chewed and discarded like mollusks in the eastern tide? I take, for example, the pride of the sufficient few, twisting like barnacles in the storm and I am left with wonder, to wonder this: if I circumscribed myself to the knowledge that I am my own content, is my being bearably enough? You could only restore a land once the graves have been accounted for. That is the content driving our lives to insurance.

Art

art is a
> human propulsion
>> and the realm of aesthetics
>>> bluebells of boundless imagination.

a challenge
> exists in the image
>> and who knows just how high
>>> the ceiling is
>>>> but the artist.

This poem first appeared in Sketch Magazine, Iowa State University, 1982.

Palm Jewel

Daphne
    under a parasol
        points me to the rain
first kiss derailment
    haunts me
no jagged tides
    just a calla lily of champagne
        coursing through my mind.

This poem first appeared in Sketch Magazine, Iowa State University 1981.

22 | Welcome *to* Flowerville

Walls

Walls. Four walls. Unbroken with polyurethane. Sneakers needing to be laced; an energy drink squeezed from hibiscus waiting to be imbibed. My solitary duty, like the roads of this city, awaits. I sit huddled on the floor, in a corner, the courageous spirit I once possessed now a fluttering insect, struggling, riding a wave of discretion, a millennia of improvement gone in one breath. Muscles canopy over stringent bones; the delay exists, my attempt denied by a thoroughly suffered ghost seeking redemption amongst four perfectly anchored walls.

The View from Taksim Square*

We are pro human, pro freedom, pro innocence seeking the truth with the inexorable thirst that we are pro knowledge, pro rights, pro dignity, and understand those who deserve freedom, devoid of subjugating oligarchs binding them to frenzy, slitting their growth. Istanbul, we believe in you and us. We are pro unity and won't digress as the truncheons beat us, tear gas flows like rivers in our protest. We see the blood, the bonfires, the stench of animosity, your crocuses and tulips in flames. We are young, watching the shadows fall. Some we'll embrace, some we can't erase, some we've yet to face, malice forever in our way.

*Turkish site of riots against deforesting Gezi Park, 2013.

Welcome *to* Flowerville | 25

What Use Have I?

What use have I for loud alarms and hyacinths at workplace farms? What use have I for ticking clocks, ill-mannered flocks and loading docks? Of course, no boss I shall discourse to toss across this moss of floss; but still endeavor, I do best, beneath this orb my head to rest.

Rude Impermanence

He is a rake, she surmised. *Nothing more or less.* And yet, as I casually contemplated her, realized she felt the thorns of his neglect, the utterances of his patronizing dictum, the teasing he was notorious for. She wanted him, was sure he felt the same, but slowly, came to acknowledge, like a proud heliotrope, his resistance to chance. Unalterable, brash messenger of impertinence had him mysteriously in its iron grasp. She sought to cast him from her mind but every waking moment brought a galaxy of unbearable torment. Oh, how she wanted to hate him. Oh, how her emotions failed her so.

Where's the Rise & Shine Brew?

MJ, have you ever seen coffee making itself? Chop! Chop!

About *the* Author

Robin Ray, formerly of Trinidad & Tobago, resides in Port Townsend, WA. He is the author of *Wetland and Other Stories* (All Things That Matter Press, 2013), *Obey the Darkness: Horror Stories*, the novels *Murder in Rock & Roll Heaven* and *Commoner the Vagabond*, and one book of non-fiction, *You Can't Sleep Here: A Clown's Guide to Surviving Homelessness*. His works have appeared at *Delphinium, Bangalore, Squawk Back, Outsider, Red Fez, Jerry Jazz Musician, Underwood Press, Scarlet Leaf, Neologism, Spark, Aphelion, Vita Brevis,* and elsewhere.

Made in the USA
Middletown, DE
28 July 2019